A Wisley Handbook

Weed Control in the Garden

RICHARD CHANCELLOR

Cassell

The Royal Horticultural Society

THE ROYAL HORTICULTURAL SOCIETY

Cassell Educational Limited
Villiers House, 41/47 Strand
London WC2N 5JE
for the Royal Horticultural Society

First published 1988
Second edition 1994

British Library Cataloguing in Publication Data
A catalogue record for this book is available from the
British Library

ISBN 0-304-32039-0

Photographs by Long Ashton Research Station,
Photos Horticultural, Harry Smith Collection,
Dennis Woodland

Line drawings by Mike Shoebridge

Phototypesetting by RGM Associates, Lord Street,
Southport, Great Britain
Printed in Hong Kong by Wing King Tong Co. Ltd.

Cover: Rosebay willowherb is a lovely but irritating weed
Back cover: Japanese knotweed is one of the largest and most
troublesome garden weeds
  Photographs by Photos Horticultural
Frontispiece: *Taraxacum officinale*, the dandelion, is one of
the most common weeds
  Photograph by Harry Smith Collection

Contents

1
Introduction

The concept of weediness is hard to define because it varies with location and with the views of the observer. One of the most useful definitions is 'a plant growing where it is not wanted'. This implies both that a plant is not necessarily always a weed and that any plant could be a weed. The kindest definition is that of the poet Emerson: 'A weed is a plant whose virtues have not yet been discovered'.

Gardens are most unusual habitats, not only because plants, which in nature would not be found growing together, are planted side by side, but also because areas of bare soil are maintained. Weeds delight in trying to colonize these areas and so the struggle is on. It is often a one-sided battle favouring the weeds, which are vigorous and competitive, over the ornamental plants or vegetables, which are more delicate or slower growing.

Some gardeners like a perfect garden, others are not too particular, but the vast majority try to keep the garden tidy with variable success, which often depends on the local weed population. A few give up the struggle completely, or never try, and have a patch of weeds, which is often the cause of trouble to their neighbours. It is best to compromise. Try to prevent weeds seeding or spreading, but don't waste time removing every single weed as it appears. To obtain maximum benefit from a garden you must be able to sit down and admire its beauty or productivity.

Some weeds are relatively innocuous, others anathema. Some are rare intruders, others, like groundsel, are found in virtually every garden. The important thing is to know your weed, its name, its strengths and its weaknesses. Then you can employ the most suitable methods for its control.

The weeds in this handbook are the worst ones – mainly perennial – that occur in gardens. If you cannot find your weed in this book, then be glad that yours is not one of the worst; but still seek expert advice, for any plant can become a problem given a suitable place and opportunity.

The purpose of this book is to help you identify the weeds in your

---

Hedge bindweed, a beautiful but tenacious climbing weed, instantly recognizable for its white, sometimes pink, trumpet flowers and broad arrowhead leaves garden; to give information about their characteristics and habits and how these can be exploited for their control; and to describe the methods of control available and advise which to use in various situations. Obviously, no responsibility can be taken for the results obtained from any treatment recommended in this book.

The advice given on chemical herbicides is in line with recommendations in force at the time of writing, but as the usage and availability of weedkillers is subject to change, it is essential to read the instructions on the label carefully before using any of them.

Almost any plant can become a weed, as in this wild garden

2
How to Use this Book

There are three main ways of using this book to find a solution to your weed problems:

Particular situations
If you have a weedy lawn, for example, then turn to chapter 4 and the first section, which deals with weed problems in lawns. If you are uncertain which weeds are present, refer to chapter 5. A general summary of methods of weed control is given in chapter 3. If weedkillers need to be used, details of the ones available are given in chapter 6 and methods of application in chapter 7. Similarly, if you have general weed problems in other areas of the garden, then turn to the appropriate section in chapter 4.

Particular weeds
If, however, you have just one weed which is over-running the garden and becoming intolerable, turn first to chapter 5 to identify it or, alternatively, look through the illustrations; then read the entry for it, which gives details of its occurrence, how it spreads and how to control it. Different methods of control can be found in chapter 3 and, if required, the herbicides available are described in chapter 6 and how to apply them in chapter 7.

Particular chemicals
If a particular chemical is required to control your problem weed, turn to chapter 6, which gives details of each weedkiller, its type of action and where it can be used. Methods of application are in chapter 7.

3
—— Methods of Weed Control ——

There are several ways of killing weeds. The most satisfactory method will depend on how the weed spreads, the numbers in which it is present and where it is growing in the garden.

Weeds are either annual, reproducing themselves from seed, or perennial. It is essential to kill annual weeds before they seed, for most produce vast numbers of seeds and a small proportion of these may survive for several decades in the soil. The adage 'One year's seeding means seven years' weeding' is only too true. There are, in any case, many seeds in garden soils. A weedy garden of one tenth of an acre (484 sq yds) could contain up to 10 million weed seeds in the soil, or roughly 20,000 per square yard. In suitable situations about 5 per cent of these will germinate in any year to give around 1,000 weed seedlings per square yard, leaving 19,000 to emerge in subsequent years, even if no further seed is shed.

Opposite: *Ajuga reptans* 'Burgundy Glow' and juniper form an impenetrable ground cover, smothering weeds and making it difficult for weed seeds to settle
Below: Like most annual weeds, scarlet pimpernel produces seeds which last for many years in the soil

Most annual weeds are relatively easy to control, if you catch them in time, by hoeing or hand weeding. Plants which are seeding should always be burnt. Those with brittle stems or tough root systems can prove more troublesome and may require treating with weedkillers. For killing established annual weeds, the most practical weedkillers are contact in action, e.g. paraquat with diquat, while germination can be controlled, in some situations, with soil-acting weedkillers.

Perennial weeds seed too, but it is their root systems which cause most trouble. Unlike annual weeds, perennnials have well-developed roots or stolons (stems) underground from which they can spread rapidly. Not only are the roots usually difficult to get at, but they must be entirely removed or killed to prevent new plants regenerating from pieces left behind in the soil. (For the same reason, it is wiser not to put perennial weeds on the compost heap unless they are thoroughly dried out first). This is where modern herbicides have proved especially valuable, enabling the gardener to deal with problem weeds more efficiently and less laboriously than by traditional methods.

HOEING

The hoe is marvellously effective in flower and vegetable beds if used properly. There is a variety of hoes available, basically divided into those you push and those you pull or chop. Hoes are ideal for controlling annual weeds and should be used before they are seeding. Some perennial weeds are also vulnerable, but those with deep roots or underground stems are usually checked only temporarily and other methods will probably be needed.

For best results, weeds should be hoed on a good drying day, when they will die quickly. They should be cut off at about soil level, so that the stems are separated from the roots. It is important to keep the hoe sharp and to use it frequently, or at least whenever a fresh crop of seedling weeds emerges.

DIGGING AND FORKING

A spade is a useful tool for ridding a plot of annual weeds. By neatly inverting blocks of soil, you can bury the weeds at a depth from which they cannot emerge and where ultimately their decayed remains form useful compost. However, this only works if the soil is fairly heavy and cohesive. On very stony soil, the weeds cannot be effectively buried and must be forked out. Burial is most successful with immature annual weeds, but if weeds such as couch grass or ground elder are present, careful forking out is essential. Remember to let the underground parts dry out thoroughly before disposing of them on a compost heap.

Hoary plantain forms a tight flat rosette of leaves

ROTARY CULTIVATORS

Mechanical cultivators can be useful in a garden where large areas of ground, especially vegetable plots, are under cultivation and where mainly annual weeds occur. They are most effective for killing weeds on drying days, but are best not used on perennial weeds, such as couch grass, which can regenerate a new plant from every piece. They may also be helpful in the first stages of clearing a neglected site, although subsequent growth will have to be treated with weedkillers or by other means.

WEEDKILLERS

Herbicides have now become accepted by the majority of gardeners as useful 'tools' in the garden. They save time and labour, especially in a large garden, and in some instances they offer the only possible solution. There is also evidence that plants grow better when weedkillers are used, because the soil is not disturbed as it is by hoeing or digging. Understandably, however, a number of gardeners still resist the use of chemicals, believing that they are poisonous to themselves or their pets or contrary to nature. Weedkillers available to gardeners are perfectly safe if used as directed, although of course are toxic to plants. They are often remarkably effective: it is vital to read the label carefully before use and to follow instructions exactly. Some weedkillers are total and will kill all plants; others are selective and will kill certain sorts, which allows for a variety of uses in different parts of the garden.

As said before, the hoe is really all that is needed for most weeds in a small garden, other than in lawns and in paths, but there are weeds and situations where a weedkilling chemical is essential for satisfactory control. Weedkillers provide an excellent solution for stoloniferous weeds in places where it is not feasible to dig them out – couch grass growing in a rock garden, for example, or perennial sow thistle in a lawn. The important thing is to make sure that the product you buy is suitable for the area in which you wish to use it. Weedkillers for paths should not be used on lawns, for instance, nor lawn weedkillers on rose beds. (See chapters 6 and 7 for details of weedkillers and how to apply them.)

CUTTING DOWN AND MOWING

Nothing is quicker and more obvious than using a sickle on a clump of nettles or a pair of shears on a patch of creeping thistle, but nothing is less effective in the long term, because they will quickly grow again. Unless one is prepared to do it regularly, cutting should be reserved for annual weeds and then with a hoe at ground level.

Mowing a lawn is similar: it cuts off the dandelion heads and plantain spikes, but does not kill the plants themselves. Many perennial lawn weeds have flat rosettes of leaves which escape the mower's blades and so they persist indefinitely. Cutting over perennial weeds is usually no more than a temporary clean-up.

HAND WEEDING

It is always a great temptation to pull out annual weeds, because they stand up and invite attention. Unfortunately, many of them have weak stems, which break and leave the roots in the ground with the lower stem leaves attached. Groundsel is notorious for this. It is best to wait until the weeds are quite large but not yet seeding and then grasp them as near the ground as possible. In heavy soils weeds come out most easily when the soil is damp. With tufted grasses, it is often simplest to hand-pull them in early spring, after many of their roots have died in the winter.

MULCHING

Mulching is an increasingly popular method of controlling weeds, even if it is not always successful with perennial ones. Grass

Lettuce mulched with chipped bark

Opposite and above: A variety of mulches: strawberry plants with straw and tomatoes with black polythene sheeting

clippings have long been used for the purpose and many other materials are suitable for smothering small weeds, including leaf-mould, rotted compost, straw and, more expensively, shredded bark. In vegetable plots, black polythene sheeting is widely used. Although it encourages weed seeds to germinate underneath, the seedlings quickly die from lack of light. It also keeps the soil moist and warm, which attracts slugs and slug pellets should be scattered beneath. A mulch is normally applied in spring to warm moist soil, which should be previously cleared of weeds, and is spread in a layer 2–3 in. (5–8 cm) thick.

GROUND COVER

Competition from ornamental plants is another way of suppressing weeds or preventing them becoming established. It is essential to rid the soil of all perennial weeds before planting the groundcover and it may be two or three years until it becomes fully effective. (For further details and recommended plants, see the Wisley Handbook, *Ground Cover Plants*.)

15

Creeping thistle has very prickly leaves and purple flower heads

4
Weed Problems in Particular Situations

For details of the weedkillers mentioned, how they act and where and when to apply them, see chapter 6.

LAWNS, PADDOCKS AND ORCHARDS

Weeds in lawns are probably the most obvious in a garden because they disfigure an area which is flat, open and supposedly uniform grass. To control weeds in lawns or rough grass by hand or hoe is difficult and tedious, although it is worth forking out isolated weeds before they spread.

Fortunately, there are a number of selective weedkillers, as they are called, which will kill the broad-leaved weeds in an established lawn without harming the narrow-leaved grasses. Many lawn weeds, especially dandelions and daisies, are readily controlled by products containing 2.4-D or MCPA, but more resistant weeds like white clover and lesser trefoil need the addition of other chemicals such as dichlorprop, mecoprop and dicamba. Lawn weedkillers have various combinations of these chemicals to control virtually all the weeds of lawns and rough grass, although some weeds will require repeated spraying at intervals. Slender speedwell is one of the most resistant.

In addition to these liquid products, applied by watering can or sprayer, there are ready-to-use aerosols and solid sticks for spot treatment of odd weeds. Many combined weedkiller and fertilizer products are available for lawns, to kill the weeds and encourage the grass.

The worst problems of lawns are patches of coarse grass or the grass-like field woodrush. These narrow-leaved weeds cannot be selectively controlled by weedkillers and have to be cut or forked out of the turf or killed by a grass-killing chemical such as glyphosate, and the area then re-seeded or re-turfed. Field woodrush can be checked to some extent by light liming, applying ground chalk or limestone at a rate of 2 oz per sq. yd (67 g per m^2) in winter.

Lawn weeds should be treated when they are growing strongly in late spring or early summer. The soil should be moist, but the grass

Daisies, clover, speedwell and dandelions are ubiquitous lawn weeds

should be more or less dry and rain not expected for at least six hours. Do not apply a weedkiller immediately after mowing and do not mow for at least three days after treatment. The grass cuttings should not be used for mulching, but composted for several months before the compost is used.

Newly sown or turfed lawns should not be treated for about six months, as the grass could be damaged. Although weeds will appear along with grass seedlings after sowing a lawn, most annual weeds will be topped and prevented from seeding by early cuts with the mower. If seedlings of difficult perennial weeds occur, such as docks, it is worth winkling them out by hand at an early stage.

Moss is a frequent problem in lawns. It is usually symptomatic of excessive shade, bad drainage, impoverished soil or incorrect mowing and can be reduced by correcting these conditions. Some gardeners like a little moss, for it is soft and pleasant to walk on and usually does no harm. However, certain mosses, notably *Polytrichum* species, which are indicators of very poor acid soils and resemble diminutive pine trees, can progressively kill areas of grass.

Moss can be controlled by various products. Lawn sand has long been used for this. Dichlorophen is another contact mosskiller, killing only what it touches, and like lawn sand is quick-acting. Chloroxuron, which is slower-acting, is usually mixed with ferrous sulphate or dichlorophen to give them a more persistent effect. Mosskillers can be applied in spring or autumn. The moss should be raked out after two to four weeks when it is dead or dying and the grass should be encouraged by applying a fertilizer.

Proper cultivation of the lawn will help prevent the recurrence of moss and improve the quality of grass generally. This can be achieved by aerating and scarifying the turf, regular feeding from spring to autumn and mowing with the blades set high enough not to scalp the grass. A healthy well-managed lawn should be easier to keep free of moss and weeds.

FLOWER BEDS AND VEGETABLE PLOTS

In the average small garden, the hoe is the best way of controlling weeds, especially in straight rows of vegetables. A mulch of black polythene can also be used among the vegetables. In a herbaceous border, where hoeing is more difficult, perennial weeds should be carefully disentangled from ornamental plants during the routine lifting and dividing in autumn or spring.

Of the herbicides available, the paraquat with diquat mixture is suitable for both flower and vegetable beds. It is a contact weed-killer, killing all green parts of plants, and must be kept off cultivated plants. It is effective against annual broad-leaved weeds and grasses, but perennials may well re-grow since only the tops are killed. As well as being directed on to weeds growing among flowers and vegetables, the mixture can be used before cultivated plants have emerged or after they have been cut down, for instance,

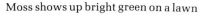

Moss shows up bright green on a lawn

Left: An overgrown rock garden being reclaimed with the use of glyphosate
Right: A mulch of straw manure among shrubs

among bulbs and herbaceous plants like paeonies or in asparagus and artichoke beds. Paraquat with diquat is also useful for cleaning up a bed which has been prepared for sowing or planting.

Glyphosate is a similar herbicide in that it will kill any plant treated. It is particularly suitable for control of perennial weeds (and indeed annual weeds too) in vegetable and flower beds, for it is taken in by the weed and carried through to the underground roots and stems, which cannot otherwise be dealt with. It is inactivated rapidly on contact with the soil and will not harm the roots of nearby plants. It is obtainable in liquid or in gel form; the latter can be painted on to individual leaves or shoots of weeds without affecting the cultivated plants and is excellent for dealing with weeds in awkward places, within vegetable rows or clumps of perennial plants, and also for tree seedlings.

As opposed to these non-selective herbicides, alloxydim sodium is a selective weedkiller which kills only grasses (apart from annual meadow grass and red fescue) and can be sprayed over flowers, shrubs and bulbs with impunity. It is especially useful against couch grass growing in a rock garden, border or other difficult spot.

ORNAMENTAL TREES, SHRUBS AND ROSES

Mulching and ground cover are good methods of suppressing weeds under ornamental trees, shrubs and roses. Annual weeds growing in bare soil can be controlled by careful hoeing, or by leaf-acting weedkillers such as glyphosate or paraquat and diquat.

Perennial weeds are best controlled by glyphosate. Dichlobenil, another soil-acting or residual herbicide, will also control a wide range of annual and perennial weeds. It should not be used under certain plants, such as larch, elder, snowberry and some hollies, which may be harmed by it. Details of usage are supplied by the manufacturer. Application should be made only in early spring when trees and shrubs are still fully dormant and they must be well established and at least two years old. The weedkilling effect lasts for about three to six months. Any weeds that do subsequently appear should be controlled with glyphosate or paraquat and diquat without disturbing the soil, which could lead to further weed emergence.

FRUIT

Mulching is a good method of weed control around fruit trees, fruit bushes (currants, gooseberries) and cane fruits (raspberries, blackberries, loganberries). Of the weedkillers, glyphosate or paraquat with diquat can be used around fruit bushes, although great care must be taken that the herbicides do not touch the cultivated plants or suckers emerging between rows. Dichlobenil granules can be scattered around established (planted for at least two years) apples, pears and fruit bushes, but not plums, cherries and strawberries, to control overwintering annual weeds, suppress some perennials and control weed seed germination for several months.

In strawberry beds, it is difficult to avoid the plants with leaf-acting weedkillers and hoeing is the only safe method. A mulch of black polythene or straw is an alternative.

PATHS, DRIVES AND PATIOS

On hard surfaces and paved areas, the absence of garden plants makes chemical weed control eminently suitable and consequently there are many products available. Most are mixtures, containing ingredients such as aminotriazole, 2,4-D, MCPA, and paraquat with diquat, which will kill existing weeds, while for longer-lasting effects more persistent weedkillers like atrazine, simazine and diuron are added. Total weed control in these situations can also be obtained and maintained with dichlobenil granules, ammonium sulphamate and sodium chlorate. You should make certain that no trees or shrubs have their roots under the treated area and it is advisable not to use weedkillers on steep slopes, as some of them, particularly sodium chlorate, can move in the soil. Odd weeds can be treated individually with glyphosate or dichlobenil.

5
Identification and ───── Descriptions of Weeds

HOW TO IDENTIFY YOUR WEED

For the purposes of this book, weeds have been identified in three
main ways – flower colour, leaf characteristics and other features.
If your unknown weed has flowers of a certain colour, say yellow,
start with the section on flower colour; then, using the list below of
those having yellow flowers, look through the appropriate entries
on individual weeds or the illustrations until you find the right one.
If no flowers are present, refer to the sections on leaf characteristics or other features of weeds and follow the same procedure.
The letters with numbers (A1, A2˙ etc.) are a key to the weed
descriptions (pp. 23–50), which are given in alphabetical order of
the botanical name.

Flower colour

Flowers white: A1, A2, C1, C3, C4, C5, C10, G1, L1, P2, P5, S3, T3.
Flowers white with yellow centre: B1.
Flowers yellow: P2, P5, R1, R2, R3, S1, S2, T1, T2, T4.
Flowers green: A3, C7, E1, P2, P3, R4, R5, U1.
Flowers pink: A1, C1, C10, E2, O1, P4.
Flowers red: R4, R5.
Flowers purple: C2, C6, C9, P1.
Flowers blue: C8, V1.
Flowers brown: L2.
Never has flowers: E3. (See also the two sections below.)

Leaf characteristics

Grasses and grass-like leaves: A3, E1, L2, P3.
Leaves long and narrow but not grass-like: C6.
Leaves divided into many narrow segments: A1, C3, R3.
Leaves divided into three or more leaflets: A2, C4, O1, R2, T2, T3.

Creeping bellflower has large fleshy roots like white carrots

Leaf margins with coarse teeth or lobes: C7, C8, C9, R2, R3, R4, S1, S2, T1, T4.

Leaf margins with shallow teeth or lobes: A2, B1, C2, E2, L1, P1, P2, R1, R5, T2, T3, U1, V1.

Leaf margins without teeth or lobes: C1, C3, C5, C6, C10, G1, O1, P4, P5, R3, R4, S3.

Leaves in opposite pairs on the stem: C5, L1, S3.

Basal leaves forming a rosette: C3, P2, R1, R2, R5, T1.

Leaves bluish green in colour: C7, C8, S2.

Leaves large: A2, P1, P5, R5, T4.

Leaves shiny and dark green: B1, R1.

Leaves like an arrowhead in shape: C1, C10, R1.

Leaves with stinging hairs: U1.

Leaves prickly to the touch: C9.

Leaves noticeably hairy: C5, L2.

No true leaves, only spindly branches: E3.

Other features

Creeping underground parts which give rise to new shoots: A1, A2, C1, C6, C8, C9, C10, E1, E3, L1, P1, P5, R3, R4, S2, T4.

Stems creeping along the soil surface: A3, C1, R2, T2, T3, U1, V1.

Producing small bulbils: O1, R1.

Very small: C3, R3, V1.

Climbing or scrambling: C1, C10, G1.

Seeds or seedpods long and narrow: C4, C6, E2, R3.

Stems containing milky juice: S2.

Weedkillers may be the best remedy for annual chickweed, because of its germination capacity

Only the worst weeds common in gardens have been included in this book. Many familiar annual weeds have been omitted, because most of these are relatively easy to control by hand-weeding or hoeing. However, if you have a particular problem weed and cannot find it here, you should seek professional advice.

DESCRIPTIONS OF WEEDS

For full details of the weedkillers mentioned, see chapter 6.

A1 *Achillea millefolium* Yarrow

Yarrow is a weed of lawns, paddocks and orchards. It increases both vegetatively and by seed. In lawns, mowing prevents flowering and seeding, but the weed spreads horizontally by slender underground stems, which grow slowly and turn up at the tips to produce new plants. Flowering, when allowed, occurs from June to September and many seeds are produced.

There are many weedkillers available for lawns, but unfortunately yarrow is not very susceptible to them. Those containing 2,4-D or MCPA with dicamba. dichlorprop, mecoprop or other additives will give some control, although treatment will need to be repeated. In dry conditions, parent plants can be hand-pulled when flowering, which may extract the underground stems as well.

Left: A young yarrow plant with finely divided leaves
Right: Ground elder has flat-topped clusters of white flowers

A2 *Aegopodium podagraria* Ground elder

Ground elder can occur almost anywhere in the garden. Like many problem perennial weeds, it relies more upon its underground stems than on seed for spread. It is usually passed between gardens by pieces of stem lodged among the roots of ornamental plants. So do look a gift plant in the roots!

Control can be difficult, but glyphosate is effective and is particularly useful in the gel form, which can be painted on individual leaves of the weed when it is growing in awkward places among garden plants. Alternatively, dichlobenil granules can be sprinkled where this weedkiller is safe to use. Both treatments will have to be repeated. Careful digging, where this is possible, will remove most of the underground stems, for they are never very deep, but watch for re-growth from missed pieces. Constant hoeing also helps, but it is at best a slow way of reducing an infestation.

A3 *Agrostis stolonifera* Creeping bent

Creeping bent occurs frequently in lawns and flower beds. It flowers in July and August and seed is often produced. However, the main means of propagation is by stems running along the surface, which can grow over 3 ft (90 cm) long in a season.

In lawns, it causes little trouble except when growing out at the edges, which should be trimmed regularly to prevent it encroaching on flower beds. Of the weedkillers, glyphosate is very effective and alloxydim sodium can be used when the weed is among growing ornamental plants.

Creeping bent is a grass with narrowly triangular leaves and usually purple stem nodes

Many people find daisies endearing, but they can be a problem on lawns

B1 *Bellis perennis* Daisy

The daisy is restricted to short mown grass or the sides of tracks and is one of the most frequent weeds of lawns, growing on all types of soil. It is a perennial weed and spreads both by seed and by slow vegetative increase of the clumps.

Daisies are very susceptible to weedkillers for lawns, of which there are many, and can be readily controlled by them.

C1 *Calystegia sepium* Hedge bindweed

As the name suggests, hedge bindweed is usually found in hedges, among fruit bushes and along fences, which all lend support. It is commonest in southern Britain. It is a perennial with extensive underground stems. Some of these emerge as new shoots each spring, their tips growing back into the ground to form new underground stems in autumn, while other stems creep horizontally through the soil and remain hidden. Hedge bindweed can form seed, which is able to survive many years buried in the soil, but in general produces little or none.

Control is not always easy, especially as the weed is relatively resistant to many weedkillers available to gardeners. Where digging is possible, the underground stems can be forked out. It is fairly susceptible to glyphosate and to many weedkillers for lawns, but when climbing up other plants the only solution is to paint individual leaves with the gel form of glyphosate.

C2 *Campanula rapunculoides* Creeping bellflower

Creeping bellflower was originally introduced as an ornamental plant and was quite widely planted in gardens until its invasive behaviour was realized. It spreads both vegetatively and by seed. The far-creeping roots can produce new shoots at a distance from the parent plant. It flowers from June to September and viable seed is produced in abundance.

Creeping bellflower can be controlled by carefully digging out the carrot-like roots, which should be dried and then burnt. Seeding must be prevented because the seeds can survive several years in the soil. There appear to be no reports, as yet, regarding its response to weedkillers but in open ground glyphosate should be effective; it may need to be applied several times as new plants will occur from seed. Dichlobenil granules can also be used where this is safe.

C3 *Capsella bursa-pastoris* Shepherd's purse

This weed can occur in all situations in the garden, flower beds, lawns, paths, waste places, etc. An annual weed, it can germinate in any month of the year and some seed can germinate as soon as shed.

It is easy to control by hoeing or in a late stage by hand pulling, but it is important not to allow seed to be shed. It is susceptible to weedkillers where these can be used.

C4 *Cardamine hirsuta* Hairy bittercress

Hairy bittercress is destined to become the number two garden weed after ground elder. It occurs in most nurseries and garden centres, where it is often seen growing in the plant containers, and is thus imported wholesale into gardens. The reasons for its increasing success lie in its very short life cycle and its explosive seed dispersal mechanism, which flings the seeds out for 3 ft (90 cm) in all directions. The seeds can germinate in most months, although seedlings appear mainly in summer or late autumn. It is often confused with *Capsella bursa pastoris* Shepherd's purse.

As soon as you see a plant, uproot it or kill it, for in a few days it will have shed its seed. This must be prevented at all costs, for with its generous seed production and short lifespan, it can quickly colonize the whole garden. In flower beds and other cultivated areas, glyphosate or the paraquat and diquat mixture are effective, but be careful to avoid your ornamental plants.

Shepherd's purse, showing distinctive heart-shaped seed pods

C5 *Cerastium holosteoides* Common mouse ear

Mouse ear is quite common in gardens, where it can be a nuisance in lawns and in flower and vegetable beds. The plant flowers from April to September and, as a perennial, produces a prodigious amount of seed year after year. The seeds can survive several decades in the soil. They germinate mainly in the autumn with only a few in spring, unlike most weeds.

Mouse ear can be controlled with most lawn weedkillers, especially those containing mecoprop, dichlorprop or dicamba. In flower beds and among vegetables, it is easiest to hoe it out, but this should be done in time to prevent seeding. It is susceptible to most weedkillers for paths and drives.

Common mouse ear has hairy leaves and stems growing along the ground or making dense hummocks

C6 *Chamaenerion angustifolium* Rosebay willowherb

Rosebay willowherb frequently establishes itself on bare untilled soil and can become a considerable pest. It grows in many places, especially gardens and among ruined buildings, and is often found on burnt-over ground, whence the name fireweed. The plant will quickly colonize an area by means of shoots arising from the creeping roots. The light and multitudinous seeds are very effective at spreading it over a distance.

Rosebay willowherb can be dug out with a fork if the soil is not too heavy, for the creeping roots do not penetrate deeply. Where weedkillers can be used, glyphosate is successful, particularly in the gel form if the weed is growing among garden plants. Dichlobenil granules can also be applied in certain situations. (See front cover.)

C7 *Chenopodium album* Fat hen

Fat hen is an annual weed which can occur in large numbers, for its seed production is prodigious especially when growing on soils rich in nitrogen. The seed germinates throughout the growing season from February to October.

Young seedlings are easily destroyed by hoeing and any that are overlooked can be hand-pulled later as the stems become tough, but those with developing seed should not be composted. Dense populations can be sprayed with glyphosate, diquat with paraquat or glufosinate-ammonium where these can be used.

C8 *Cicerbia macrophylla* Blue sow thistle

Blue sow thistle was introduced as an ornamental plant for its attractive flowers. However, it rapidly invades and can take over whole gardens, including lawns, paths and flower beds. It spreads entirely by the far-creeping underground stems, which produce a mat of roots and exclude other plants. It is presumably passed between gardens by pieces of the underground stems being transplanted, either deliberately or accidentally, along with other plants.

Left: Rosebay willowherb grows up to 4 ft (1.2 m) high
Right: Blue sow thistle has blue-green leaves and light blue flowers on tall slender stems

Blue sow thistle can be forked out relatively easily as the creeping stems do not go deep into the soil. If completely removed, there will be no reinfestation owing to the absence of seeds. Its response to herbicides is unknown, but where digging is impossible, for instance, among cultivated plants, then glyphosate as a directed spray or in gel form should be effective. In grass, weedkillers for lawns should be successful.

C9 *Cirsium arvense* Creeping thistle
Creeping thistle is one of the most frequent perennial weeds, growing in cultivated ground and grassland, roadsides, waste places and often in gardens. It produces masses of conspicuous thistledown, which is of no importance, for it very seldom has seeds attached. The most important means of increase is by the creeping roots, which give rise to new shoots away from the parent. These very brittle roots are virtually impossible to dig out completely and any fragments left behind can regenerate new plants.

Digging and hoeing the weed is generally ineffective and it is best to use a weedkiller. In grass, it can be controlled by any lawn weedkiller, although more than one application may be necessary. In flower beds, glyphosate gel may be applied and dichlobenil can be used around certain established trees and shrubs.

C10 *Convolvulus arvensis* Field bindweed
Field bindweed is a persistent weed which occurs in many habitats, particularly gardens. It likes undisturbed situations where it can proliferate by the roots and is also favoured by warm dry conditions, which encourage seed production. It is most widespread in England and Wales. The plant flowers between July and September, but forms seed only in hot summers. The seeds have hard impervious coats, which enable them to survive for up to 30 years in the soil. To the gardener, it is the creeping roots which are important. Places where the weed is well established are full of the slender roots growing through the soil and producing new shoots at intervals.

As with most weeds which have regenerative roots, it is a waste of time trying to dig them all out, especially as the vertical ones can go as deep as 20 ft (6 m). Where safe to do so, glyphosate can be used, either as a spray or, in difficult situations, in the gel form painted on individual leaves. In lawns, most lawn weedkillers will be effective. It can also be controlled or checked by dichlobenil.

E1 *Elymus repens* Couch grass
Couch grass is very common and the bane of many gardeners. It is

a vigorous plant and forms ever-increasing clumps. The tips of the underground stems give rise to shoots in autumn or spring, which grow rapidly and very soon start new underground stems from their base. These too grow rapidly and spread through the soil.

Control is relatively simple. The stems can be dug out, if the soil is not too heavy, for they are shallow and do not break easily. Of the weedkillers, glyphosate will kill couch grass completely at any time of year when in active growth. Among ornamental plants, the selective herbicide alloxydim sodium can be sprayed. It is best applied when the weed is growing strongly in spring, has five to six leaves on the shoot and is 6–12 in. (15–30 cm) high.

E2 *Epilobium montanum* Broad-leaved willowherb
Broad-leaved willowherb is one of several willowherbs which can be troublesome (in addition to the grander rosebay willowherb). It spreads vegetatively and by seed. Short creeping stems produce small rosettes of leaves in the autumn, which grow into the new flowering stems in spring. The plant does not creep far, but forms

Left: Field horsetail and creeping thistle. Field horsetail produces brown fertile shoots with small cones at tips, followed by green sterile roots
Right: Field bindweed twines around other plants, to 4 ft (1.2 m) high

clusters of daughter plants. The seeds, which are very light, can be carried great distances and germinate in both spring and autumn.

The weed can be dug up or hoed over, but you must ensure that no creeping stems remain alive. Glyphosate or paraquat with diquat should kill it, although it is resistant to many other herbicides.

E3 *Equisetum arvense* Field horsetail

Field horsetail usually occurs in large patches and is often found in gardens, where it constitutes a serious problem. The spores which reproduce it are small and generally able to establish new plants only in moist situations. Once established in a suitable place, the plant spreads from underground creeping stems growing deep in the soil. These produce small tubers, yellow when young, which can give rise to new plants as can fragments of the stems themselves.

Field horsetail is difficult to eradicate and very resistant to herbicides. Most will simply kill off the stems above ground, which re-grow later from the subterranean parts. Dichlobenil, where it can be used, will help suppress the weed, as will sodium chlorate.

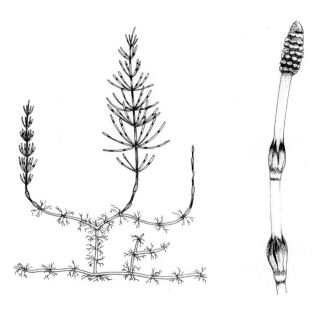

Field or common horsetail with sterile stem and (right) a fertile stem

Left: Broad-leaved willowherb reaches about 2 ft (60 cm) tall, with small pink flowers
Right: Annual goosegrass, or cleavers, with its delicate flowers

Glyphosate also gives some control, but repeat doses will be needed. Weedkillers may have greater effect if the stems of the weed are bruised before treatment.

G1 *Galium aparine* Goosegrass, Cleavers
Goosegrass is an annual weed that germinates in autumn and winter and so is often well established by the start of the growing season. In gardens it occurs frequently in hedges and in shrubberies.

Goosegrass growing among bushes can be removed by hand-pulling when the stems are 2–3 ft (60–90 cm) tall. They then break off at ground level and do not later regrow, providing useful compost if no seeds are present. Seedlings of young plants in cultivated ground are easily hoed out.

L1 *Lamium album* White deadnettle
White deadnettle inhabits waste places throughout Britain,

particularly England, and is also quite common in gardens, where it can be a nuisance in flower beds. It is superficially similar to a stinging nettle, but does not sting. Propagation is mainly by the stout, white, creeping, underground stems with numerous tough roots.

The weed is difficult to dislodge from flower beds by digging without damage to the ornamental plants. It is also resistant to many weedkillers. Mature plants can be controlled with glyphosate, but repeated applications will probably be necessary. Dichlobenil granules can be used where it is safe to do so for seedling control.

L2 *Luzula campestris* Field woodrush

Field woodrush is almost exclusively a weed of lawns and other grassland which is poor in nutrients. Although it flowers, the constant mowing of lawns usually prevents the formation of seeds. Its main method of spread, once established, is by short creeping stems.

Control in lawns is very difficult because it is resistant to all the weedkillers suitable for lawns. One solution is to spot treat the

Left: White deadnettle has large white flowers, much more conspicuous than those of the stinging nettle
Right: Field woodrush is a grass-like plant which forms a rosette of broad hairy leaves, from which arise brown flowers on 6 in. (16 cm) stems

weed with glyphosate and, when it is dead, to re-seed the area with grass. Another possibility is to cut out the whole plant with a spade and then re-turf or re-seed. Light liming (see p. 17) can be useful in reducing acidity and the build-up of thatch, which are favourable to the plant.

O1 *Oxalis corymbosa* and *O. latifolia* Pink-flowered oxalis

There are two pink-flowered oxalis which cause serious problems in gardens. Both were introduced as ornamental plants and are now widespread in gardens, nurseries and glasshouses. They are quite frequent in southern England, with *O. corymbosa* being most plentiful around London and *O. latifolia* in the southwest. Although oxalis flower abundantly, no seed is formed and they increase solely by means of bulbils. In *O. latifolia* the bulbils are on short stalks, while in *O. corymbosa* they are stalkless. Dispersal of the weed is almost entirely due to digging, for the bulbils stick to boots and spade and are quickly transferred to other parts of the garden.

Control is difficult once the plants are established. It is probably best not to try digging them up, although a few people claim to have

Bulb and bulbils of
Oxalis corymbosa

eliminated the weed in this way. It is said that piglets will root out and eat the bulbils, but the animals are likely to do more harm than good to the garden. The only treatment is to paint or spray the leaves of oxalis frequently with paraquat and diquat or glyphosate, to exhaust the food reserves of the bulbils. Never put bulbils on the compost heap: burn them or dispose of them elsewhere.

Left: *Oxalis corymbosa*, frequently found around London
Right: *Oxalis latifolia*, found mainly in the southwest. Both these introductions
are difficult to control. The pink-flowered oxalis are up to 1 ft (30 cm) high, with
leaves divided into three heart-shaped leaflets and attractive flowers

P1 *Petasites fragrans* Winter heliotrope

Winter heliotrope was introduced in 1806 as a winter-flowering
ornamental plant. It was widely grown and the leaves were used in
the cut-flower trade. It is not very hardy and so it is commonest in
the south of England where, in the milder districts, it thrives and
can become a weed. The flowers open between December and
March and do not always survive the winter. It spreads entirely by
the underground stems, which in warm counties, such as Devon
and Cornwall, can grow rapidly.

Where digging is possible, control is quite easy, the creeping
stems being relatively shallow in the soil. In flower beds,
glyphosate gel painted on the leaves is effective. On paths and
drives, sodium chlorate, dichlobenil and other weedkillers suitable
for paths will give good control.

P2 *Plantago major* Greater plantain

Greater plantain is the commonest of the three perennial plantains
(the other two being ribwort plantain and hoary plantain) and
always grows in open ground. In gardens, it is frequent in lawns,
but also occurs in flower beds and borders. It is unusual among
perennial weeds in that it can flower and set seed in its first year. It

flowers from May to September and has been recorded as producing an average of 14,000 seeds per plant per year, which can survive for several decades in the soil.

As the leaves lie very flat on the ground, close mowing is no cure for this weed in lawns. However, like the other plantains, it is susceptible to all the weedkillers suitable for lawns and is therefore easily controlled. In cultivated soil it may be simply forked out or killed by hoeing.

P3 *Poa annua* Annual meadow grass

Annual meadow grass is a small, tufted, annual grass which is one of the most frequent weeds of gardens, growing on paths, in flower and vegetable beds and in lawns. Its prevalence is explained by the fact that it can flower and set seed and the seeds can germinate in every month of the year. It also produces many seeds – an estimated average of 8,000 per plant – which are able to survive several years in the soil.

The weed is difficult to kill by hoeing unless conditions are very dry. In cultivated soil, glyphosate or paraquat with diquat are very effective, as is dichlobenil where it can be used. Simazine will kill germinating seeds on paths and drives. All weedkillers suitable for paths are successful.

Left: Greater plantain carries spires of yellowish white flowers above the rosette of leaves
Right: Annual meadow grass bears a roughly triangular flower head, green or tinged with purple

P4 *Polygonum aviculare* Knotgrass

This annual weed occurs quite frequently in flower beds and vegetable plots and occasionally on paths and drives. It germinates only in spring from February to May and once established is very hard to pull up, thus is sometimes called Ironweed.

In flower beds and in vegetables it should be hoed out when very young. On paths and drives weedkillers for paths are effective.

P5 *Polygonum cuspidatum* (Fallopia japonica) Japanese knotweed

Japanese knotweed was introduced as a garden plant in 1825 and was subsequently widely planted. It is one of the largest garden weeds in this country. It is now naturalized in an extensive area around London, in southwest England, in Wales and in southwest Scotland and is said to be spreading rapidly in some western counties. The weed flowers from July to October and seed, when it is formed, remains dormant in the soil for a few years. The main method of increase is by the stout, reddish, underground, creeping stems, which emerge in February and March to produce new shoots and continually spread outwards.

The plant is difficult to keep under control, especially in shrubberies along stream banks and other moist places favourable to it. When increasing rapidly, it is advisable to kill the colony completely. The most effective weedkiller is glyphosate, especially in September, but repeated treatment will be necessary and care must be taken to avoid contaminating streams or spraying ornamental plants.

R1 *Ranunculus ficaria* Lesser celandine

Lesser celandine is found in grassland, woodland, hedgerows and along streams; in gardens, it can grow almost anywhere. There are two forms of the weed, one producing seeds, the other producing bulbils in the axils of the leaves. The latter is the most frequent in gardens. The bulbils are small plants with a bud and a root, which quickly establish themselves when shed. Both forms can also re-generate from the root tubers.

In flower beds and borders, the tubers and bulbils can be carefully dug out or glyphosate can be used. On paths and drives, the weed-killers for paths are effective. In lawns, lesser celandine is hard to deal with as it is not very susceptible to weedkillers for lawns. However, repeated treatment with those containing MCPA will give some control. If only small areas of lawn are infested, it may be best to kill the weed with glyphosate and then re-turf or re-seed.

Left: Annual knotgrass should be hoed out when young
Right: Japanese knotweed is up to 9 ft (3 m) tall, with generally reddish stems
which are hollow between the nodes, like thick bamboos; the broad leaves are
cut straight across at the base, distinguishing it from its garden relatives

R2 *Ranunculus repens* Creeping buttercup

Creeping buttercup is generally a weed of grassland, especially
low-lying wet ground and ditches. In gardens, it is a nuisance in
lawns and can rapidly invade flower and vegetable beds too. It
spreads principally by the creeping stems, which run outwards in
all directions during the summer to produce new daughter plants
at intervals. The plant flowers from May to June and, if not cut
down, produces only about 150 seeds per plant, although these can
survive for many years in the soil.

In lawns, creeping buttercup is readily controlled by all weedkillers suitable for lawns. In cultivated ground and on paths,
glyphosate or paraquat with diquat are very effective. Young
creeping stems may be hoed successfully, but mature plants need
digging out.

R3 *Rorippa sylvestris* Creeping yellow cress

Creeping yellow cress is almost always confined to nurseries and
gardens. It prefers lighter soils, but is very persistent. Although it
flowers in abundance between May and August, few seeds are

41

Left: Lesser celandine has glossy, dark green, heart-shaped leaves and bright yellow flowers
Right: creeping buttercup has deeply lobed leaves and flowers on stems up to 2 ft (60 cm) high; a notorious weed, although a rare old form used to be grown in gardens.

produced. The plant spreads mainly by shoots arising from the far-spreading roots.

The root system is impossible to dig out, for it is thread-like, difficult to see and pieces remaining in the soil will readily re-generate new shoots. Its response to many weedkillers is not known, but glyphosate or dichlobenil should be effective, where they can be used.

R4 *Rumex acetosella* Sheep's sorrel

Although sheep's sorrel is common on acid soils, it also grows on neutral ones. In gardens, it is a weed of lawns, flower beds and rock gardens, where its creeping habit is not always noticed until too late. It is one of a small number of weeds which can give rise to new shoots from any part of the extensive root system. In addition, the flowers, which open from May to August, sometimes produce seeds.

Most weedkillers for lawns will give some control of sheep's sorrel in grass, but repeated applications may be necessary. In very acid conditions, two useful deterrents are a light dressing of lime for lawns (see p. 17) and a mulch of mushroom bed compost among shrubs and in herbaceous borders. Glyphosate is also effective in flower and vegetable beds. Digging out the creeping roots completely is difficult and hoeing results in further but weaker re-growth.

Sheep's sorrel has two distinctive lobes at the base of each leaf

R5 *Rumex crispus* and *R. obtusifolius*
Curled and Broad-leaved dock

Curled dock and broad-leaved dock can be troublesome in areas of turf or rough grass, such as orchards and paddocks. Reproduction is mainly by seed. Large plants are able to produce up to 30,000 seeds a year, some of which can survive up to 80 years in the soil. Pieces of taproot can regenerate new plants, but only from the top portion.

In rough grass, weedkillers suitable for lawns will have some effect but, as the weed grows resistant with age, repeated applications will probably be required. Around shrubberies, glyphosate can be used. If only a few plants are present, it is worth spudding out the top 4–6 in. (10–15 cm) of the taproot. In newly sown lawns, hand weeding of seedlings can save trouble later.

S1 *Senecio vulgaris* Groundsel

Groundsel is one of the commonest weeds of gardens and one of the most irritating to gardeners, for the seeds come in continually on the wind over the garden fence. It grows just about everywhere in gardens, except possibly in lawns. The reason for its great success is its seasonal adaptability. Groundsel can germinate, flower and produce seeds in any month of the year. The lifespan is short, as little as five weeks, and up to three generations can occur in a year. Each plant produces about 1,000 seeds and, if every seed of all three generations grows into a plant, then a year's progeny from one plant could number 1,000 million.

This annoying weed is small, numerous and difficult to deal with. Germination of the seeds can be prevented on bare soil by the soil-acting herbicide dichlobenil, where it can be used. Dichlobenil granules are also effective on paths and drives, along with other weedkillers suitable for paths. The weed can be hand-pulled, but usually the stems break. Hoeing may be successful in dry weather, although plants can re-root in wet conditions.

S2 *Sonchus arvensis* Perennial sow thistle

Perennial sow thistle is a common weed of roadsides, from where it distributes a lot of wind-borne seeds. As a result, it often occurs in gardens, particularly in flower and vegetable beds, although it can also become established in lawns. It is most frequent in southern Britain. The weed has two means of increase. The flowers

Left: Creeping yellow cress produces flowering shoots up to 18 in. (45 cm) high from small leaf rosettes which, in winter, are lime-green and inconspicuous
Right: A young groundsel with limp ragged-looking leaves. It will produce tiny yellow flowers, giving way to fluffy seed heads

Left and right: curled and broad-leaved dock grow up to 3 ft (1 m) tall, with heads of numerous, reddish green flowers. A young broad-leaved dock plant (right) should be eliminated as soon as it is recognizable

appear from July to October and produce many seeds – up to 20,000 per plant. In addition, the creeping roots can produce new plants throughout their length.

Most weedkillers for lawns will give good control, but more than one application may be necessary. Where safe to use, glyphosate is very effective as a directed spray or in the gel formulation; be sure to treat every rosette.

S3 *Stellaria media* Chickweed

Like Groundsel and Shepherd's purse this annual weed can germinate in any month of the year. It normally forms small much branched plants, but in moist fertile soils can produce dense lush growth.

Although the stems are feeble and easily broken, the plant is often difficult to hoe out effectively and it is best done when seedlings are small and on a good drying day, for in moist conditions young

Left: Perennial sow thistle is 4 ft (1.2 m) high in flower, with a rosette of long, narrow, coarsely-toothed leaves
Right: Dandelion is sometimes cultivated for the leaves, which are used in salads

plants can readily reroot. Glyphosate, diquat with paraquat or glufosinate-ammonium are also effective where they can be used.

T1 *Taraxacum officinale* Dandelion

Dandelions grow just about anywhere in gardens. They flower from March to October, but mostly in spring. Many seeds are produced, and over 5,000 per plant each year has been recorded. The seeds are light and have a plume of hairs on the top, which enables them to be dispersed by the wind. The taproot is very re-generative and small pieces from any level are capable of producing new plants.

If the whole roots can be dug out, this is a good way to control the weed in cultivated soil, but hoeing off the tops is a waste of time, for the roots quickly produce new shoots. When digging is not possible, glyphosate is very effective. In lawns, any weedkiller suitable for lawns can be applied, although treatments may have to be repeated. On paths and in certain other situations, dichlobenil granules can be used. (See frontispiece, p. 1.)

T2 *Trifolium dubium* Lesser trefoil

Lesser trefoil is an annual weed, found mainly in lawns and close-cut grass, where it can be abundant, especially if the turf is impoverished. It can occur in other parts of the garden, but is then a minor irritation rather than a problem. The plants flowers from May to October and produces many seeds, which germinate in both spring and autumn. As the leaflets are small and grass-green and the leafy stems creep out sideways in the grass, it is not very noticeable in a lawn until it flowers.

It is very important to prevent plants from seeding. If only a few plants are present, the creeping stems can be lifted up to reveal the single central taproot, which can then be pulled or cut. Most lawn weedkillers will have only a limited effect, for the weed is not very susceptible. Repeat treatments will certainly be necessary and should be continued for several years, as new plants will be produced each year from seed in the soil. Mowing does not control lesser trefoil and, if it is mown when seeding, this will help distribute the seeds even more widely.

T3 *Trifolium repens* White clover

White clover is a problem weed of lawns and forms obvious, dark green patches, which can be difficult to mow when luxuriant. It relies mainly on vegetative increase, the plant growing ever outwards and the creeping stems rooting as they spread (unlike the annual lesser trefoil). It can produce seeds, which are capable of lasting 20 years in the soil, but regular mowing will prevent this, as the flower heads are erect and vulnerable.

Control is always difficult. Although most lawn weedkillers will have some effect, especially those containing dichlorprop or mecoprop, white clover is not very susceptible to them and repeated applications will be needed. Mowing does no more than check the outward growth of the plant and it is virtually impossible to hand weed in lawns. Dense areas can be thinned by raking to lift the stems before mowing.

T4 *Tussilago farfara* Coltsfoot

Coltsfoot is fortunately not often a weed of gardens, but when it does occur, it can be a great problem, especially in heavy soils. It is a perennial weed, with thick, fleshy, underground stems which creep extensively. In addition, the flowers, which appear from March to May, produce many seeds. These are light and have a plume of hairs for dispersal by the wind. The seeds have no dormancy and will germinate at once in suitable conditions,

Left: *Trifolium dubium* produces flowers of pale yellow, turning light brown
Right: White clover has clusters of small white or pinkish flowers

although they are exceptionally shortlived and only capable of germinating in the four months after shedding.

In uncultivated areas glyphosate is effective, but may have to be applied more than once. Dichlobenil also gives good control. It is possible to dig out the underground stems in light soils, but any remaining pieces will give rise to new plants. On paths and drives, sodium chlorate and products containing aminotriazole will help suppress the weed.

U1 *Urtica dioica* Stinging nettle

In gardens, the perennial stinging nettle usually grows in paddocks, orchards and other areas of rough grass, especially those high in phosphate, such as around derelict buildings. (The annual nettle, on the other hand, is mainly a weed of cultivated soil and is distinguished by its much smaller size and white, as opposed to yellow, roots.) The weed has two methods of spread – seeds and surface-creeping stems. When both sexes are present (they are on separate plants), seeds can be produced in large numbers and are capable of surviving several years in the soil. The creeping stems run along the surface of the soil, rooting as they go, and in spring their tips turn up to produce new flowering shoots.

In rough grassland, the weedkillers suitable for lawns will control nettles, but repeated applications may be required. Dichlobenil and glyphosate are both effective in other situations where they can be used. Nettles can be forked out or undercut with a spade, as regeneration from the yellow roots is rare.

V1 *Veronica filiformis* Slender speedwell
Slender speedwell is one of several garden plants which have turned out to be weeds after they were introduced. In the 1920s it

Left: Coltsfoot has broad angular leaves, usually emerging after the flowers
Right: The stinging nettle has noticeable hairy, stinging leaves and insignificant green flowers

Slender speedwell has kidney-shaped leaves and delightful, bright blue flowers

was widely planted and then spread to other gardens, waste places an occasionally churchyards. Fortunately, it does not form seed. However, its creeping ability is considerable and, once in a garden, it will rapidly invade every part. It is also spread by cut-off pieces of stem, which re-root in damp conditions and may be carried and dropped by nest-building birds. (By contrast, most other speed-wells common in gardens are annual weeds and easy to check.)

Slender speedwell in lawns is difficult to control, although lawn weedkillers containing mecoprop are said to have some effect after several applications. Where safe to use, glyphosate and paraquat with diquat will kill the weed, while these and other suitable weed-killers will control it on paths and drives.

6
Chemicals Available for Weed Control

There are a number of proprietary products available for weed control in gardens, based either on single chemicals or more often on mixtures of chemicals. It is important to know something of their characteristics to obtain greatest benefit from them. The chemicals are listed here, as on the container labels, by their common names. These can be confusing, so make sure you have the correct one.

The list includes most of the major weedkilling chemicals currently approved for use in gardens. It does not give the proprietary products themselves, as these may change both in content and in brand name. However, the chemical constituents are always shown on the label of the product, together with details of application. These instructions must be read carefully before using any weedkiller, for it is absolutely essential to use it in the right situation, under the right conditions and in the right manner.

Weedkillers are classified as 'total' or 'non-selective', killing all plants present (e.g. sodium chlorate); and 'selective', killing certain plants only and not others (e.g. 2,4-D). Most selective weedkillers distinguish between broad-leaved weeds and grasses, being toxic to one and not the other. Many are used on lawns, except for alloxydim sodium, which controls most grassy weeds among flowers and shrubs. Most other weedkillers are non-selective, but some can be made selective by the method or time of application. Dichlobenil is used at low dosage rates, remaining in the top layer of soil. Paraquat with diquat is physically directed on to particular weeds while avoiding ornamental plants, or is applied before they appear. Total weedkillers like sodium chlorate are non-selective to such an extent that they destroy all vegetation and sometimes other forms of life as well, including insects and bacteria.

Weedkillers are applied in two ways, either to the leaves of the weeds, or to the soil, and are therefore described as 'leaf-acting' or 'soil-acting'. Leaf-acting herbicides, which enter weeds through the leaves and stems, are further divided into two types, 'contact' and 'translocated', according to how they work. Contact weed-killers (e.g. paraquat and diquat) kill only the green parts of the plant – foliage and stems – which they touch and are then inactivated and do not normally persist in the soil. They produce rapid results and can be used at any time of year when weed growth is evident. Translocated weedkillers (e.g. glyphosate) penetrate and move within the plant to kill the invisible underground parts as well. They take effect more slowly and should be applied when the weeds are growing vigorously and their food reserves are low.

Soil-acting herbicides (e.g. simazine) are absorbed by weeds through the roots and transmitted to the parts above ground. They are also termed 'residual' and remain in the soil for weeks or months, killing germinating weeds and in some cases checking established ones too. They must be applied to clean bare earth, without a weed in sight. Accurate dosage is essential, since they are influenced by such variable factors as the weather and texture of the soil.

A number of herbicides are more complex and combine different modes of action – leaf-acting with soil-acting, for example. However, these broad categories are a helpful guide to their basic characteristics.

LIST OF WEEDKILLERS

Alloxydim sodium

This is a selective weedkiller which kills grasses (except annual meadow grass and red fescue) and does not harm broad-leaved plants. It can be sprayed over shrubs, roses, bulbs and flowers without damaging them and is especially useful against couch grass in flower beds and shrub borders. It is best applied when grass growth is active, between April and September, and is most effective on couch-grass when the shoots have five to six leaves (see p. 32). The chemical is quickly broken down in the soil and does not persist. Be careful that spray does not drift on to lawns, ornamental grasses or sweet corn.

Aminotriazole

This total weedkiller is available only in combination with other chemicals, for use on paths and drives and uncultivated waste places. It kills most weeds, which turn white or pinkish white before dying. As it persists for only about one to two months, it is frequently mixed with simazine, which lasts the whole season and kills germinating weed seeds. Thus the ground is cleared by aminotriazole and kept free of weeds by simazine or other added weedkillers.

Ammonium sulphamate (NOT sulphate)

This is especially useful when reclaiming neglected areas, for it will kill brambles and most woody weeds. It is also used on paths. Only unplanted ground should be treated, where there is no risk of damage to tree and shrub roots. It is a total weedkiller like sodium chlorate, but less persistent, remaining in the soil for about three months. It is corrosive to some metals, so use a plastic sprayer or watering can.

Ammonium sulphate   See lawn sand (p. 56)

Atrazine

Sometimes included in weedkiller preparations for paths and drives, as it is similar to simazine, atrazine kills weed seeds as they germinate, while other chemicals in the mixture kill existing weeds. It is relatively insoluble and persists in the soil for most of the season.

Chloroxuron

This mosskiller for paths and lawns is usually mixed with other chemicals. The effects last for up to two months.

2,4-D

This is one of the commonest constituents of lawn weedkillers and of lawn weedkiller and fertilizer mixtures. It is a selective herbicide which controls many of the most frequent weeds of lawns, such as dandelions and daisies, but not the more resistant ones, like white clover, for which other chemicals are usually added.

2,4-D is also included in products for the control of brambles, sycamore saplings and similar woody weeds and large rank patches of weeds like stinging nettles and thistles in neglected areas.

Dalapon

Dalapon is used principally on paths, drives and vacant land for the control of annual and perennial grassy weeds, including couch grass. Repeat applications may be necessary for well established perennial grasses. Mainly a translocated herbicide, it is most effective when applied to the leaves of strongly growing grasses. However, it is taken up by the roots as well as by the leaves and persists for up to eight weeks in the soil. It should not therefore be used where there are underlying tree or shrub roots and no planting should be carried out for at least eight weeks after treatment.

Dalapon can also be used in the dormant season around fruit bushes and apples and pears, which must be over three years old. Plants should be protected from accidental contact and the spray must be carefully directed, applying only enough to wet the foliage of the weeds and avoiding run-off into the soil. In cultivated ground, alloxydim sodium and glyphosate are probably safer alternatives.

Dicamba
Widely combined with 2,4-D as a lawn weedkiller, this helps kill weeds such as yarrow and white clover which are inadequately controlled by 2,4-D. The same mixture can also be used for coarse weeds and tree saplings in uncultivated land.

Dichlobenil
This is available in the form of granules to control many perennial and annual weeds and to kill germinating ones. It can only be used around most ornamental trees and shrubs (consult manufacturer's list), roses, fruit bushes and apples and pears, all of which must be well established, that is, planted two years or more. Dichlobenil should not be used near bulbs, annuals or herbaceous plants, nor around greenhouses. It is applied in winter or early spring to clean moist earth and is locked into the top layer, persisting for three to six months as long as the soil is not disturbed by hoeing or digging. It is not recommended for light sandy soils. Do not apply when foliage is wet, in case granules lodge in the leaves of garden plants and cause damage.

Dichlobenil is also used at higher dosage rates on paths and drives and is particularly good for spot treatment of weeds growing in cracks between paving stones.

Dichlorophen
This is a quick-acting contact mosskiller for lawns, paths, drives and patios, used on its own in mixtures with other chemicals, fertilizers and fungicides.

Dichlorprop
This selective herbicide is frequently combined with 2,4-D as a lawn weedkiller, to check difficult weeds such as yarrow, white clover and lesser trefoil which are inadequately controlled by 2,4-D.

Diquat See paraquat with diquat.

Glyphosate used to clear the ground around a small tree

Diuron
A residual weedkiller, this is mixed with other chemicals such as simazine to give total weed control on paths, drives, patios and similar situations for a whole season or longer.

Ferric and ferrous sulphate
These mosskillers are available alone or combined with other chemicals for use on lawns. Fertilizers are often added so that the

whole lawn can be treated, avoiding the deep green patches which can result from application to small areas.

Glufosinate-ammonium

This is a non-selective weedkiller used for killing unsightly weeds on paths, drives and patios. It can also be used on weeds between trees and shrubs, along fences and for initial clearing of ground before planting, but keep it clear of garden plants. It breaks down naturally in the soil, but there are restrictions in the number of treatments per year around fruit trees and bushes and before planting edible crops (see the instructions). Best results are obtained on dry days when the weeds are growing fast.

Glyphosate

This is one of the most valuable weedkillers in gardens, for it is extremely effective on most weeds and does not persist in the soil. It is particularly useful against difficult perennial weeds with deep or brittle roots, such as ground elder, field bindweed and even field horsetail, and also against grasses, especially couch grass. However, it is not selective and will equally kill all cultivated plants with which it comes in contact. It should be applied to perennial weeds between early July and mid-September, when the foliage is actively growing or the weeds are starting to flower, although couch grass can be treated in any season. Most persistent weeds may need several applications. Glyphosate is available as a liquid or in a gel formulation, which can be painted on to individual weeds in inaccessible places. It is a translocated herbicide and relatively slow to act, taking three to four weeks to show results. However, the ground can be planted or sown as soon as the weeds are dead. Do not use if rain is expected within six hours.

Lawn sand

This traditional remedy for moss in lawns typically contains one part ferrous sulphate to three parts ammonium sulphate, with fine sand as a carrier. It should be applied in autumn or late March to early April, at a rate of 4 oz per sq. yd (135 g per m^2) and is most effective in warm moist conditions. If rain does not fall within a few days of application, then the lawn should be watered thoroughly.

MCPA

This is widely used with other chemicals for weed control on paths, drives and patios and for dealing with problem weeds like nettles and thistles on waste land. It is a selective herbicide similar to 2,4-D and is also an ingredient of lawn weedkillers and lawn weedkiller-fertilizer products.

Mecoprop
This selective herbicide is often included in lawn weedkillers to control difficult weeds, such as white clover, procumbent pearlwort and, to some extent, lesser trefoil and yarrow, although the last two will need repeated treatments. It is most effective when these weeds have produced flower stems and are up to the flowering stage, but no later – that is, June and July.

Paraquat with diquat
This well-known weedkiller is very useful for a fast kill of growing weeds. It can be used around trees and shrubs, fruit or rose bushes and between vegetables and flowers. It can also be applied before cultivated plants emerge or after they have been cut down, or to clean up the soil in preparation for planting. It is a contact non-selective herbicide and in all cases great care must be taken to

Lawn weedkillers often include mecoprop, for treating problem weeds like white clover

avoid any of the mixture falling on the leaves or green parts, including buds and green bark, of plants. Paraquat with diquat is particularly effective against annual weeds, but will kill only the tops and not the roots of perennial weeds (except creeping butter-cup, which is killed because it has no underground food reserves.) However, repeated applications will eventually weaken perennials. Thorough spray coverage is important and it can be applied at any time of the year, preferably when the weeds are small. It is not affected by rain after treatment as it is very fast-acting. The weeds start to dry up within 24 hours and no residue is left in the soil, so that sowing or planting can be carried out almost immediately. For safety, the mixture is sold as soluble granules in measured dose sachets and is applied in the form of droplets with a sprinkle bar or fine rose on a watering can. It is not suitable for pure peat or peat-based composts.

Paraquat with diquat is also available mixed with simazine and aminotriazole for controlling weeds on paths and drives.

Propachlor

This weedkiller kills annual weeds as they germinate and so is applied to weed-free soil to prevent weeds occurring in certain sown and transplanted vegetables, annual bedding plants and also around established trees, shrubs and flowers (see manufacturer's list for suitable situations). It should be applied to moist finely tilled soil clear of weeds immediately after sowing or planting or as otherwise recommended. Soil disturbance after it has been applied will reduce its effectiveness.

Simazine

Because of its persistence, simazine is often added to products for paths and drives, mixed with one or more of several other chemicals, which either kill existing weeds or enhance simazine's control of germinating weeds. It is particularly good in these situations, being less likely than some other weedkillers to creep into the surrounding soil. Nevertheless, the tolerance of nearby plants should be checked.

Sodium chlorate

Sodium chlorate is the traditional garden weedkiller. It is available either alone or mixed with atrazine, for use on paths, drives and

Winter heliotrope can spread on to paths, where it may be controlled with sodium chlorate patios and for clearing neglected land. It kills all vegetation very quickly, leaving it in a highly inflammable condition, and is therefore formulated with an added fire depressant. It is very soluble and can be washed sideways, especially on slopes, and could kill plants adjacent to the treated area. It should not be used where there are underlying tree or shrub roots. It persists in the soil for four to 12 months, depending on soil type, season and weather conditions. Sodium chlorate is corrosive to metal and it is advisable to use a plastic sprayer or watering can.

Tar oil
This is available in preparations for dealing with moss, mould and slime on paths, patios, hard tennis courts and walls.

Field bindweed can be checked by dichlobenil

7
—— How to Apply Weedkillers ——

For the average garden where few weedkillers are needed, a watering can fitted with a small rose or, better still, with a dribble bar is probably sufficient. It is simple to use and lessens the risk of spray damage. For the larger garden, a pressure sprayer is helpful and especially when using soil-acting weedkillers, which require very accurate application. A sprayer has the advantage of producing many fine droplets, giving regular and uniform coverage of weed leaves, whereas the coarser drops of a watering can tend to give less even treatment and can roll off the foliage. However, there is always a danger, even in light winds, of spray drifting on to garden plants and harming them. It is a wise precaution when spraying to protect nearby plants with polythene or screen them with a piece of board.

In addition to liquid concentrates, weedkillers are available as powders or grains to be dissolved in water. Others are sold as granules, which are sprinkled on the soil surface. The best way to do this, on a small scale, is to punch holes in the lid of a jar, fill it with a dose of granules calculated for the area to be covered and then shake it as evenly as possible over the measured area. On a larger scale, a special wheeled distributor may be necessary.

Weedkillers can also be obtained in the form of solid sticks which are dabbed on individual weeds, and ready-to-use 'guns', or hand sprayers, and aerosols, some containing marker foam to show which weeds have been dealt with. There is also the handy gel form of glyphosate for spot treatment of weeds.

All products available to amateurs have been cleared under the government's Control of Pesticides Regulations 1986 for safety to humans, domestic animals and wildlife when used in accordance with the instructions on the label. The law states that only approved pesticides (insecticides, fungicides and herbicides) may be supplied, stored and used. Further, it divides them into two categories – those approved for farmers, growers and professional horticulturalists on the one hand and those for home gardeners on the other. It is now illegal for amateurs to obtain, or use, commercial products intended for professional use. (For details of the new regulations and a list of approved products, with both chemical and brand names, see the booklet, *Directory of Garden*

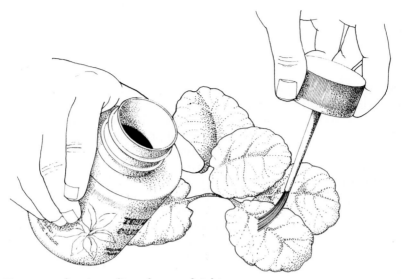

Two types of spot weeding, above and right

Chemicals, issued by the British Agrochemicals Association Ltd.)

It is most important to read the label carefully, not only to observe the precautions printed there, but also to ensure that the weedkiller is suitable and approved for the particular situation where you want to use it and to follow the instructions for dilution and application. Accurate application is essential, especially with soil-acting herbicides. Carefully follow the instructions, which usually stipulate a measured quantity of weedkiller in a certain amount of water to treat a specified area. It is a good idea to practise first with plain water, to see whether the recommendations are realistic and whether you should increase or slow down your walking speed.

There are several basic rules to follow when using weedkillers. You should have a separate watering can or sprayer reserved exclusively for them. Paint 'weedkillers only' on the side. Wear rubber gloves and fill the can or sprayer outside in the garden and not at the kitchen sink. Only mix up sufficient for immediate needs; it is better to make more spray if needed, than to dispose of an unwanted surplus. If there is any left over, don't store it but apply to a gravel path or other uncultivated area, choosing a place well away from ponds, ditches and water sources, where there is no risk of contamination or seepage. Never be tempted to put in extra

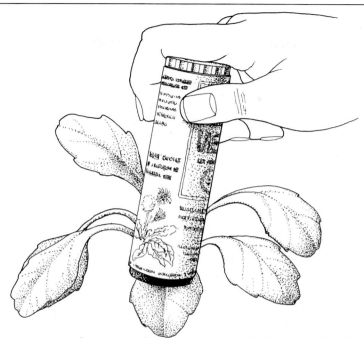

concentrate to get better results, as stronger solutions may be less effective or, conversely, could cause serious damage. Rinse out the container very thoroughly so that there is no residue.

Weedkillers should always be kept in their original labelled packaging, tightly closed. They should be stored out of reach of children and pets, preferably in a locked cupboard, and in a frost-free place (not in the greenhouse, however, and not near food). Place empty containers in the dustbin and get rid of any old containers which have lost their labels in the same way.

As far as application is concerned, never spray in windy weather. In particular, take care to prevent spray drifting on to neighbours' plants. Weedkillers generally should not be applied in extreme conditions, such as drought or frost, nor in bright sunshine, which may result in damage to garden plants. Try to avoid spraying when bees are active and make sure that pets are out of the way until the spray has dried.

Remember that some weedkillers are very rapid in action, while others are slower and may take weeks before they show the full effects. So, just because nothing happens in a few days, do not assume that a treatment is not going to work. Do not be worried by weedkillers: used correctly and sensibly, they can be a very useful aid to gardeners.

Index

Page numbers in **bold** refer to illustrations